MW01107129

Li'l Bastard

128 Chubby Sonnets

David McGimpsey

Coach House Books | Toronto

copyright © David McGimpsey, 2011
first edition

Canada Council for the Arts Conseil des Arts du Canada

Canadä

Published with the generous assistance of the Canada Council for the Arts and the Ontario Arts Council. Coach House Books also acknowledges the Government of Ontario through the Ontario Book Publishing Tax Credit and the Government of Canada through the Canada Book Fund.

LIBRARY AND ARCHIVES CANADA CATALOGUING IN PUBLICATION

McGimpsey, David, [date]
Li'l Bastard / David McGimpsey.

Poems.
ISBN 978-1-55245-248-6

I. Title.

PS8575.G48L55 2011 C811'.5 C2011-904944-9

for Lynn

I. St. Lawrence Street

1. Re: Report to the Council, cc The Huffer Foundation *et al.*

At last year's prestigious Ho-Lit awards
I won the coveted Layton Medallion
(rhymes with 'Canadian stallion'), now nestled
in my chest hair as I winter in Crete.

So, *mes chères*, not that you're sleeping,
wondering which Doritos Collisions
will collide next, but you are well served –
I thank my editor, Minka, &c.

Hard at work on my mystery novel now:
Murder Most Murdersome, You Murder-Maker.
I'm hoping to wake one day to say, 'It was
all a dream – those poplar-moon poems!'

The glare of my medallion, however, is real.
Real as the beatings administered behind
the Mont St-Antoine arena. Those beatings
were the worst of your very harsh winters.

2. Montreal, home of the Washington Generals.

In the end, I had to go back to teaching.
Back to two-percent milk and Mopey-O's.
Back to due diligence with winter tires
and maintaining faith in Derek Jeter.

Every novel idea I have goes awry:
I end up calling the love interest 'Fabiana'
or the protagonist suddenly finds gold
in the sock meant to hold the ball bearings.

You know, going back to school doesn't mean
I've given up on living; going back
to school just means I've given up on life.
Though my clothes suggest I gave up in '92.

In the end, I had to go back to the hood –
my mien, my chow, my view *au cimetière*.
Dude, you should have been there at open mic –
I sang 'Skankland Refuge' and it was epic.

3. If you can't leave me be, then leave me alone.

I'm compelled to say I like your haircut.
Now your head's the answer to the questions
What if Lady Gaga cut her own hair
and *What if Lady Gaga were legally blind?*

Most days, I have been busy at the print shop.
I still confuse 'Wednesday' with 'the weekend.'
Are you still working on your stories?
The ones with the sour mothers being all sour?

I apologize for the way sun sneaks into
my study. I'm not sure why, but I do.
It is my sincere hope you now have a puddle
named after you and you still chew quietly.

Hey, a mug clang and old-days e-hugs
for the memories of that gyro stand, eh?
Oh, those times we said things about our friends
behind their backs! Their stupid Gap-clad backs.

4. To expedite your snooping, my e-mail password is 'abortionist.'

A glossy fashion mag boasts '300 Flirty
Looks for the New Year,' which can only mean
we're subjected to a year with sixty-five
or sixty-six unflirty days. Unacceptable!

Melville, apparently, just kept at it.
The sea, the skiffs, the scrimshaw and scrivening.
A note in a galley of *The Whale* reads:
'Ponce de Leotard: First Person Round the Panty.'

I'm saying I like the idea of sitting down
without really needing to get up again.
I'm saying I had no idea what flirt.com was –
Nina, I was in my professor clothes!

My grey sweater and blue shirt combo
will soon be featured in the slick pages
of *Grey Sweater and Blue Shirt Combo
Magazine*. Name, as always, misspelled.

5. Speaking of stealing cars and running them off into the quarry to collect the insurance money, I ran into your father. Your real father.

It's so embarrassing, the cutesy pet names
adult lovers adopt. I called her 'pookie' and 'snook'
and she called me 'horseface' and 'the human wallet.'
Oh, snook, we bought so much lawn furniture!

Then, making my plans to move down south,
I stopped stooping from the weight of that shame.
I sold my hockey cards. Even Bobby Orr.
I sold my woodcarvings. Even Bobby Orr.

Yes, money poured in like gravy at the wrap
party for *The Biggest Loser*. I thought
a red truck and a beagle named Steve
were all any sensible Texan would need.

I asked her, 'Am I being vain or stupid?'
'Sweetie, it's like when you asked if I found you
ugly on the outside or on the inside –
it really isn't an either/or situation.'

6. My Canadian Novel.

The Newfoundland orphange playground.
Then asleep in the stiff nunnery's bed.
The train was stalled at Portage and Main.
'Just around then my marriage fell apart.'

The pea garden was not just her hobby,
but a metaphor for *memory* and *loss*:
when the river ice breaks up in April,
I discover my father kept a mistress.

A journal the other woman's daughter found
in a cedar chest full of baby clothes
was the story of a woman's courage
and how a war wound kept a man alive.

In the Stamford, Ontario, archives,
a historical oddity is unearthed
and chased into Mediterranean hills –
where they've never endured a real winter.

7. Bury me beneath the willow but throw out my DVD collection – it's useless.

I tell my students Gertrude Stein did not
just wake up knowing how to punch a zebra.
You have to be dedicated to the craft.
First, you have to know how to punch a horse.

Likewise, I wanted to move to Texas,
and installing a ranch-dressing pump
in my kitchen was my inauspicious start.
Another shift of classes and I'm gone.

When I announced my intention to leave,
my friends very caringly inquired into
how to go about applying for my job.
I just said, 'You should ask Jason.'

'Jason from the English Department?'
'No, Jason Seaver, the dad from *Growing Pains* –
he's actually a real person, you know.
He's advising me to be a better friend to Boner ... '

8. Even with the kleptomania, I was the perfect boyfriend.

When I put on my silk suit and pince-nez,
I hap to think upon the treading verse
of McCawmber Hextall. 'Hush, pale stone,
there'll be no more magnets for you!'

Oh, I enjoyed the poster stand in Sears,
so much so I spent a Christmas Eve
in the juvie docket the same day I smacked
Manny Destrine just for being Manny.

I would have stolen a bedroom poster
of Carolyn Forché if I'd seen the jacket
photo from *The Country Between Us* –
I settled for Kathy Ireland all the same.

In the can, I wrote my very first poem.
The poem went, 'I know where you live, pig,'
and basically just repeated that line.
Hush, pale stone, I live in the hip Plateau.

9. Orville Redenbacher's mistress rejects the label 'porn star.'

'Who're you calling a literary hipster?'
he huffed, putting down his pint of Steam Whistle.
I apologized, of course, and promised
to read his second book, *Suck It, Dick Cheney.*

The next day I was back at the office.
The whole floor had been freshly painted –
clementine and puce – and the new mirrors
could expose the most clandestine bald spot.

I could hear that hipster from last night
crying in front of Prof. Dean's class.
I wished there were more taco stands nearby,
but no taco, they say, is worth suicide.

Who was I to diss the hipster poet?
Bowing my head into my late grading –
I've used the word 'iffy' in a reference letter.
I've cancelled two classes to watch *Survivor*.

10. You're now talking to the Sleepy's Mattress Employee of the Month.

A new study suggests affirmation chants
(i.e., *I can be loved, I can be loved*)
are generally ineffective. In fact,
they may tend to have a reverse effect.

Let's say you're about to be evicted
from your already earwig-infested room.
You have red spots on the back of your legs,
and your nickname is Lancelot Loser.

Let's say your last prized possession
is a souvenir glass from Hoboken
and your ex has just published a poem
titled 'I Know the Definition of *Small*.'

Chanting *I can be loved, I can be loved*,
only stresses how sadly untrue that may be.
It's likely better to just buy a toupee.
I can wear a rug, I can wear a rug.

11. David McGimpsey likes – then unlikes – this.

A knife in the back is just the adult
version of acne. It will clear up.
Faster, if you learn to mix gin with gin.
Faster, if you drape mirrors in burlap.

The words you wrote look good in a shredder:
'If only I didn't join that knife club!'
and 'If only I objected to adding
the phrase *I will be stabbed* to our vows.'

Acceptance is the philosophical concept
that eases long grief and allows someone
to consider tan slacks as their destiny.
That Taylor Swift song is not about you.

Healing is just a word for understanding
how I was right and you were unright-like.
Taylor Swift would not use the word 'douchey,'
and Applebee's would just ask you to leave.

12. If Jesus drove a dependable family-sized recreational vehicle, He would drive a Dodge Caravan.

Maybe I shouldn't have high-fived the priest.
Maybe it was a mistake to fall asleep
at the Don Ho anniversary show.
Still, I forgave myself at Crookback's Pub.

I invented a laptop with cupholders.
Previously, my sole innovation
had been putting my hand in my pocket
to give people the finger while they talked.

I longed for the road and the good things in life:
the warm breeze, eating chips while riding shotty,
selling rifles just over the Mexican border
to a compound of polygamists.

Those people who say you can't run away
from your problems aren't really trying.
I left my lease on St. Lawrence Street.
Off to Brownsville. *Commence-toi la gris.*

13. My second, less popular and even less critically successful Canadian novel.

The woman at the insurance company.
Georgetown, Ontario. The description
of exquisite unsaids. The turn will not
take place in an Olive Garden parking lot.

The male foil will disappear in good time,
and the mister with the disfigurement
will prove more deft with buckles. Regardless,
he or they will not just say, 'Eat it, nit.'

No mitten too far, no Béliveau too
deconstructed. 'The blue lights spilled over
the winter fields of Bowmanville as the night
offered bludgeon after bludgeon.' Sleep, sleep.

The plot thickens when the mother's file
is discovered and there are hushed hints
of New York. Just a weekend, it seemed.
Not that she really loved John Wilkes Booth.

14. Viva Smokey

Contrary to rumour, I never owned
just one suit. I had four identical suits,
each with a nickname: 'Stainy', 'Scuffers,' 'Elbows'
and 'Smokey.' I liked Smokey the best.

Smokey was the man. Smokey saw me through
nights on the couch; Smokey wrote long essays
about suicidal poets and baseball:
'Bunting Is an Art, and I Do It Well.'

Smokey saw me through the bar on Bishop,
where I danced to the ThelMo Wheat Combo,
a spirited group whose name meant 'Thelonious
Monk may be dead but we have to eat too.'

Not much could be won by my nickels and dimes,
but I moaned when I put Smokey away
and knew it was Stainy's turn in the rotation.
Now, Stainy. Stainy, he was all business.

15. As my mother was always fond of saying, 'It depends whose ox is being gored.'

Justin Bieber, someday you will grow strong
and then you will exact revenge for the pain
I experienced that Halloween night.
You know, when I was dressed as Geddy Lee.

My novel's now called *The Mistakener*
and I dutifully watch the CBC.
I mean, PBS. It's not like I killed somebody.
For my sin, I expect a pair of PUMAs.

So long Mount Royal, hello livin' in a van!
Goodbye Wendy's on Décarie Boulevard,
Hello Wendy's on Lamar Boulevard!
For my virtue, I expect more thinness.

You know what might be easier? If you
all took turns poking me in the arm
with a jagged lamb shank. Then, just maybe,
I might stop to ponder your sweet 'concerns.'

16. If possums were pears, we'd be having fruit salad tonight.

The phrase 'a grey, mechanical existence'
made me think I'd solved something painful.
It somehow upset me to discover
it was nonsense. I craved sunshine, love.

My philosophical uncle would say,
'When you're old, suicide'll seem redundant.'
Like me, he took TV shows personally
and cried at the thought of any goodbye.

At some point, the blows themselves don't hurt
anymore. You already know you've lost
and what'll really hurt is the healing pain
of tomorrow. Stupid tomorrow.

When I finally left that apartment
I didn't even quite put on my shoes.
I stepped on the heels as if they were slippers
and ran to the car taking me to Texas.

II. Perdita, TX

17. Scrubland.

A sign for a gas station sixteen miles off
is like anticipating a trip to New York.
Everything bent west from hurricane winds,
a radio tower, a flutter of starlings.

Sun-sick, still thinking of a week in May
when I wanted a silent treatment to stick.
The glum, clipped calls and a waffle breakfast
I couldn't quite sit through. Stupid waffles.

The gas station, of course, is just a gas station:
trucker-sized coffee, bags of corn chips
and local papers fourteen pages long.
Item: San Benito Soldier Killed in Iraq.

The Romans counselled *Never argue with the sun.*
Trying to not talk, happy without a phone.
Praying my eyes will survive the Texas light.
Dwarf juniper, mesquite, transplanted palms.

18. The streets of Laredo.

Discount shoes, Hannah Montana handbags,
Marlboro Lights in hundred-degree heat.
A border patrol hydrofoil combs
the Rio Grande looking for hale swimmers.

Mayoreo y menudeo. More and less.
Easy to get into Mexico, hard to get
into the U.S., harder to forget home,
expensive to rent a car out of Houston.

I had planned to smile for the whole week,
assume dolour was a Montreal flu,
but picking over silver wrestlers' masks,
toy guitars and tamarinds, the flu was back.

Impossible to look at a window
without someone asking if you need drugs
or a prostitute. The moon is red at night,
low to the river, ignorant of boundaries.

19. Sugarland.

Candy-coated pecans, Dr. Pepper,
kolaches and pure cane mints. Later,
in Houston, listening to a band play Merle,
I smile, merely grateful for Anheuser-Busch.

Sugar Land is just a place with a factory,
more gated community than foxglove field.
I ask a girl in a strip mall where the town
centre is and she says it 'doesn't matter.'

Hat pins and shot glasses. Time to decorate.
A last, persistent ember of long desire
goes out, somewhere between San Antonio
and Austin, before a show for college kids.

Metaphors of extinguishment aside,
Texas continues to blaze and I resist
SPFs 15 to 50. I have another chance:
a sour tea to swallow without sugarpop.

20. DFW.

Tortilla soup, *papas con limón*,
Shiner Bock beer. I make love to a new phone
in a Mexican restaurant just by the highway.
'You can really taste the *manteca*.'

She has a truck and I'm drunk in Fort Worth.
'I'll drive you into Dallas,' she says,
'but in the morning you have to drive us back.
Now, get me a burrito to go, Hoss.'

The poems I just 'have to see,' of course,
are too sincere a side for hotel salsa.
'The last time I saw my father alive
I pawned his high school graduation ring.'

I never do drive back into Fort Worth,
but, I should add, I sing in a band called Sage
for four weeks in a bar called Sour Joe's.
Forty bucks, a free meal and four drinks' pay.

21. Chupacabra.

I listen to you like an old employee,
waiting on official permission to leave.
You talk about friendship but I switch
to talk of the news. 'It's a mess out there.'

I start to get into *Barnaby Jones*,
that seventies cop show starring Buddy Ebsen
about a senior-citizen private eye
whose cunning foils the most pernicious men.

There's news of a *chupacabra* sighting
in McAllen. The Latino sasquatch,
chupacabra's a wolf-kangaroo combo
that lives off goat blood, just like Katie Couric.

I could talk cryptozoology all night.
I could also immerse myself in *Barnaby*.
I just can't stand being the deposed
blue suit who apologizes for the sun.

22. Palmito Ranch.

A sun-bleached post past Boca Chica, where,
a month after Appomattox, perhaps sparked
by a colonel's political ambition,
the Union lost the last battle of the civil war.

It would be dumb to compare my recent losses
to such folly. Unlike the soldiers who
died in that white-lit cane and river weed,
I've known my war's been over for years.

My battle was more like the lonely senior
unto a telemarketer, unsure how
a 'free vacation' needs two credit card
numbers. Once dug in, shame is hard to outflank.

River road, country music, *chicharrones*.
Faded shrimp boats and a handpainted sign
for 'Camaron coktal.' Stopped by border patrol.
'I'm a tourist,' I say. 'I do what I want.'

23. Sixth and Red River.

Pimply bands at Emo's, smoking out back,
girls in white shorts, cops tackling winos.
I play guitar at a garden-benefit show
and end up fighting with a customer.

I'm taken in but released on my own,
or at least before being asked for my papers.
The talk of the evening is a beauty queen
who seems to have the best grades on campus.

'Ms. Longhorn deserved the grade she got.
If y'all ask me, I don't understand
why, at rodeos and birria breakfasts,
there was so much fussing about her A.'

If arrested I would have used my phone call
to ask after Esplanade street back home.
Those slippery walks through the dark,
the mountain cross lighting my way upstairs.

24. East Texas.

Early spring phlox blossoms around the oaks.
Armadillos are back on the highways.
There's wifi at most any truck stop now.
Update: *Eighteen Wheels, A Dozen Sonnets.*

At a church supper, there's a choice of two
different meats so I choose chicken and chicken.
'You're far away,' the woman who ladles my giblet
gravy says. 'I meant the way you look, darling.'

I wouldn't know the warble of a waxwing
from the sound of a tire losing air.
But, soon enough, all I have to compare
myself to is such sustained deflation.

The state line and a pale-blue motel room.
The American Champs-Élysées:
those endless retail and resto boulevards.
Olive Garden, Best Buy and Pep Boys.

25. Aransas County.

I expect to see Ferris wheels blinking
at night, as if every coastal village
comes with its own Santa Monica Pier.
I see more familiar refinery lights.

Hurricane, a Scorpions cover band,
is playing and I'm drunk one guitar
solo in. As far as Corpus Christi
eighties cover bands go, Hurricane rules.

The only other over-forty asks me
if I fish – deep-sea, big marlin fishing.
I tell him my father was a clammer,
even though Pops worked for Gulf Oil.

Lining up with the Hurricanes themselves
at Whataburger, I hold up my phone
and shout, 'Drunk dial! Should I do it?'
For stopping me, Hurricane is the best.

26. Dinosaur Valley.

Snaposaur, Timbalasaur, Excitotops.
I know little about how dinosaurs lived
four thousand years ago. I know they wore top hats,
and loved to eyeball people in their SUVs.

I sit by the Paluxy River to mourn
the little I knew about the one I loved.
The river cuts into its limestone bed:
an ugly ravine, a trash-filled abscess.

By the grace of the Sinclair Oil company,
I've come along. Raised in a refinery town,
aware of the link between leukemia
and benzene, between payday and dime bag.

The river gorge is as mute as the dinos.
Not a clue as to who'll win *America's*
Next Top Model. She'll be a pretty one:
standing before me, unloved by the camera.

27. Over the Pecos.

The last time I talked to Rob Allen,
outside the course of his deathbed vigil
and the grievous secrets of our circle,
we talked about bridges over the Pecos.

Rob never looked far off when talking travel,
and I often left his company thinking
he had the clip of a real man: driving home
after Reno, stone broke, a smile on his face.

Rob poured drinks with elegance, talked books
as if each were under a newspaper headline,
smirked at ambition and indignity.
He knew what ate Meriwether Lewis.

Rob was cooler with how it would end than I was:
I cross the Pecos praising his Lucifer.
The glint of plastic bottles stuck in sagebrush,
writing poems only because I once could.

28. New flavours of jerky.

Seventeen flavours of jerky, just one life to live.
Night driving, lost, around Huntsville:
rabbits darting, nimrods with high-beams on.
I remain unperturbed by chili stains.

I took a room at La Quinta for five nights,
thinking I'd jack the AC and just write.
I ended up watching *Barnaby Jones*
twice a day. *Living* for *Barnaby Jones*.

I think of my first chapbook, *Li'l Chappie*,
and of scrubbing out the dedication to Erin
and writing 'Dedicated to La Quinta's
clean affordable rooms and helpful staff.'

From my suite I can see a highway billboard
for a waterpark – zoo animals wearing
inner tubes. The giraffes look neck-shackled;
the rubber tires set to bring them down.

29. Panhandle rag

Motel mirrors are a hard-to-love truth.
They make no pretence toward your heart
or your lovability. The soap bar,
wafer thin, barely absolves your road stink.

No matter where, hair salons adopt names
that pun the craft. Some vaguely funereal
and grave: *Curl Up and Dye, Cut Down in Your Prime*
and, of course, *Hair Today, Gone Tomorrow.*

In Amarillo, a man's makeover
is happily simple: you buy a new
State of Texas belt buckle and smile.
The smiling part is the most burdensome.

Some spit in your face and blame you for your
failure to turn that spit into wine.
Most walk into a mall and know what to do.
Some just lie back and watch *Barnaby Jones.*

30. The stockyards.

Whiling away at Ruby's Hot Saloon
I bore some nit with talk of *Barnaby*
and brag about my first publication –
the poetry chapbook *Li'l Chappie.*

They were all long poems about a mall.
The powdered-lemon-doughnut monologue
meant to show my upper-class masters
I knew Tennyson's *Maud* and Bea Arthur's *Maude.*

'That's cool,' my interlocutor coughs,
'and by cool I mean a complete waste of time.'
He says Texas is a Hollywood thing,
born in the lots where Tom Mix doesn't die.

'Smashing in your windows with a golf club
is also a Hollywood thing,' I aver.
I wish I wrote the song 'Half-Price Lawyers.'
'Half-Price Lawyers' transcends literature.

31. Waco.

Filing papers, telling mother I'm okay.
putting away the put-awayables.
My hand-annotated *Blithedale Romance*
now in a San Marcos secondhand shop.

There is only one book worth studying.
Cooking with Dr. Pepper. The recipe
for Dr. Pepper barbecue sauce (DPQ)
alone keeps me alive through the worst times.

There's DPQ in my glove compartment.
And you better believe there's DPQ
stacked in a tall pyramid of Mason jars
on my kitchen counter. I'm okay.

You can smell oakwood in the summer air
and as periwinkles withstand the heat,
I am ready to just lie down a while.
All the Dr Pepper I'll ever be.

32. Bluebonnets.

The room costs eighty but she pays anyway.
We eat burgers and dance to a Faith Hill song
at a roadside country bar called the Hub.
Cans of Bud till the windows light with dawn.

In the plywood suite of the La Picara
Motel, I wake up to the one who knows
how to touch my neck and who also talks
about old Warner Bros. movies.

In *White Heat*, Cagney has this business:
he shoots a guy in a car trunk but his first
concern is eating a piece of chicken.
'He's so great,' I say. 'Obvies,' she says.

Her sweet eyes, her pain about her one love
who did not think about motor lodges.
She used to lie down in fields of bluebonnets.
Now she wants to be a writer.

III. Barnaby Jones.
A Quinn Martin Production.

33. Tonight's Episode: A Footbridge Higher.

I drink milk and like to dig up interesting facts.
For example, did you know the original line
of clothing for American Eagle Outfitters
was actually made for eagles? It's true.

Did you know that Benjamin Franklin
invented the wedgie? Did you know
the first flavor of Jell-O was 'malt'?
Did you know Mussolini was Danish?

I know some people grow weary of me.
The two most common nicknames I have now
are 'The Redoubtable Gustaph' and 'Grandpa.'
When I feel bad I like to take long walks.

A crossing guard suggested I was too fat,
and retirement would never suit me.
I told him not to worry. It's a fact:
Saddam Hussein was once a crossing guard.

34. Tonight's Episode: The Insomniac Strikes A-kilter.

In the middle of the night, a mousetrap went off.
I didn't want to check it out. Hopefully
the little bugger escaped and is sitting
under the floorboards, smoking Marlboros.

When I was fifteen I was arrested
for smuggling heroin into small towns.
Seemed strange I was haunted by crafty mice
and a girl who once left me alone in a bar.

I called up Jedediah and told him to take
my cases tomorrow. 'Are you okay,
Uncle Barnaby?' he asked with concern.
I wanted to confess I was waiting for death.

Instead, I reminded him Kate Hudson
is also a world-renowned pastry chef.
'There are more things in heaven and earth, Jed.'
Eyes and ears, ears and eyes. Everything goes.

35. Tonight's Episode: Into the Tiger's Nest.

The jingle *Call 1-800-267-*
2001! Alarm Force! was sung
originally by Diana Ross. Never
too late, they say, from their EZ chairs.

But it is too late to unask Brenda Auclaire
to go see Pantera with me. Too late
to change the typos in my official memoir.
I meant *analyze*. It was a mistake.

One of the innovations the Perrabee
tribe introduced to Europeans
were the volume measures *mezzo, grande*
and *venti*. Look it up on your cup, dope.

I'm still working on that unsolved fraud case,
the one where the young man was disguised
as Falstaff. Maybe it's too late to change
but I should never forget to take my pills.

36. Tonight's Episode: False Spring, Real Fall.

My daughter-in-law was once a beauty queen.
Betty's official duties, like all Miss
Virginias, included prosecuting
the state's most incorrigible tax frauds.

So, she's been a great help on the legal end.
Unfortunately, she's been kidnapped more
times than Rod Stewart has had his hair frosted.
All the money she saves, I waste on ransom.

We both brown-bag it to the office. Tuna.
Tomato. Sometimes, I remind her how,
in my day, we'd just call people names
like 'Pegleg,' 'Stinkler' or 'Big German Sue.'

I spritz the ferns in the office and tell her
the secret to life is letting go. Love,
family, career. 'Oh, old Doc Golightly,'
Betty harrumphs, 'feed the effin' pigeons!'

37. Tonight's Episode: The Ides of Marchmain.

I walk through the alleys looking for a clue.
I write down things I see: a drooping balcony,
an abandoned cooler, Burger King wrappers.
I once thought these details made love letters.

Caesar was known to his buddies as 'Kegsy.'
The precise spot where he was stabbed by Brutus
is now the site of the only KFC in Rome.
Squirrels will wear pyjamas if you fit them right.

The concept of valet parking enrages me.
The original title of *Les Fleurs du mal*
was 'Hellzapoppin'!' but who remembers?
The alleys have no real secrets to divulge.

I've lost too many friends to count. I say
to myself, 'That's just the way God wants it,'
so often I believe it too. Then again,
I'm the one avoiding the boulevard.

38. Tonight's Episode: The Forgotten Body.

I can't explain why so many undercover jobs
end with me dancing soft-shoe routines onstage.
Even when I knew damn well Eddie Cantor
was responsible for tracking down Dillinger.

I let my son go. I let my wife go.
You will never see me crying again.
I wish I could say the same thing about
dancing. No excuse for a man my age.

Wreaths of rosemary. Crowns of sage.
I see people on all those late-night ads
for weight-loss plans and just want to die.
The main ingredient in yogourt is jelly.

The tap in my feet is still around,
long after the desire to move that way
left me. At least with people around. When
it's just me and the mice, I'm Disco King Bee.

39. Tonight's Episode: The Mountains Wait Like a Lady, Like a Very Special Mountain Lady They Wait.

I am too old to be waiting for a name
to pop up on my screen. Too old to compare
the music of the Outlook Express inbox
to an arpeggio on a saintly harp.

Harpists always seem so virginal.
If a harpist told me she wanted
to pay her way through college turning tricks
I'd say, 'Straight to heaven, blessed MFA!'

The music in the torn clouds is one thing,
as is having lunch with an attractive woman.
But I am not too old for that other waiting,
that other harp-playing on one side of the hills.

A nurse says, 'Come this way,' so angelically
I'm surprised she doesn't take my hand.
'I'd love to,' I reply, rehearsing, because
when it's for real I'll want to play it right.

40. Tonight's Episode: Funeral for a Funeral Home.

My father lived until he was a hundred.
His heart and muscles outliving his senses,
completely deaf and blind by the end. 'It's
lonely,' he said. 'Can't even watch the ballgame.'

I tried Tai Chi. I am proud of my hair.
Almost everything people say to me
now ends with the phrase 'for a man your age.'
In my family, the mind is the last thing to go.

Did you know that Mikey from the Life
cereal ads was a young Philip Roth?
Did you know the Constitution's preamble
was originally sixteen limericks?

There once was a squire from Massachusetts ...
Fuck. I would have described L.A. Dodgers
games to my dad, if only he could hear.
Regret is not an issue for a man my age.

41. Tonight's Episode: Lethal Over-the-Counter Medicine.

The facts – the way I saw them – excused me.
Fitzgerald had a pet mule named Donny,
so why shouldn't I? Patton invented
the bong hit, so how could things be that bad?

You'll never see me mooning over a car,
you'll never see me in O'Rourke's again.
Did you know distiller José Cuervo
coined the terms 'paradigm shift' and 'manscape'?

Anything worth doing, as you may well know,
must come with a commemorative plaque.
After discovering the polio vaccine
Jonas Salk invented hot-air popcorn.

What's the act of 'letting go' when the body
is telling you, every morning, *soon enough?*
I can tell you, in private Rich Little
mostly did impressions of Lucille Ball.

42. Tonight's Episode: Trouble in Little Armenia.

Mata Hari died a virgin. Fresca
is responsible for most juvenile crime.
I signed a petition to change the name
of Encinitas to Big Condorville.

Not everything is on the up and up.
Once, I really tried to simply walk away
and concentrate on golf, but the same
sadness I sought to flee was what brought me back.

I knew the kind of friendship people wanted:
when they needed a reference they could count
on me, and when I needed to be reminded
I wasn't attractive I could count on them.

I go to Zankou Chicken twice a week.
I use the word 'mature' instead of 'old.'
Which reminds me, in Renaissance England,
'little death' meant 'pretentious asshole.'

43. Tonight's Episode: The Angel Sleeps in Burbank.

I'd love to say I've solved all my cases,
but some files remain open. My main error
was not relying on 'gas-station wisdom'
but depressive procrastination. Two years.

Sherlock Holmes was based on a puppet show.
Agatha Christie wrote all her novels
on tablecloths. I kept believing I would
get to *The Case of the Glass Heart*, but I didn't.

You never know how the failure of love
will rip you. You never know how bliss
does much the same. Once, on a catamaran,
I waited until she sobered up to kiss her.

These days, I'd just pour her a jigger of gin
and wave from the dock. I'd go home
and read from *Spain: Corporate Villain*,
too tired to follow even the obvious leads.

44. Tonight's Episode: Tweedle-Dee-Death.

I easily accept that one might rather
watch *Mrs. Doubtfire* than hang out with me.
The original script for *Mrs. Doubtfire*
was the last work penned by William Faulkner.

So many Hollyweirdos. So little
money for meth. Maybe I will return
to finally sort the freaks from the superfreaks.
Maybe I'll just sit in a bathrobe.

Terry cloth was the preferred fabric of Emily Dickinson;
muslin was the preferred fabric of De Sade.
Everybody is wrapped up in something,
some are cocooned for their entire lives.

My old tap shoes sit in my office closet,
shiny and black. My autographed portrait
of JoAnne Worley – 'Love ya, Barnaby!' –
was destroyed in a suspicious fire.

45. Tonight's Episode: The Eyes Lie Twice.

A fist through the drywall. A souvenir bat
from Louisville, hard ash, lying on the bed.
I'd always had time for taking fingerprints.
Now, suddenly, it seems like a waste of time.

The Roman god Mercury, ironically, hated
mortals who predicted the weather. Ann Landers
never could take advice, no matter how sound,
and she spent nights making prank calls to England.

I am in the age of ointments and creams.
Sometimes I make it out to the cake district
(around Fairfax) but a good night's sleep
reminds me renewal (not change) is possible.

One of Rumi's less-quoted adages
is 'Don't brag about your odometer.'
Meaning, I imagine, no matter how far
you go you're nowhere and you're nothing.

46. Tonight's Episode: Springtime for Schemers

Twitter was founded in the 1920s
by Charleston Twitter III. When a woman
orders an 'all-dressed gyro' she should call it
'gyra.' Spring robins really hate the Dutch.

I started to get into bread. White, brown,
pumpernickel, rye – it didn't matter.
Playing the parts of both lonely old man
and park pigeon, I tore off two years.

There's a Montreal bagel place on Beverly
where I banged out most of my memoirs:
'Being both a private detective
and a senior means great gun savings.'

Double latte. Avocado cream cheese.
I'm not a stylist but I did discover one phrase
that could make anything seem insignificant –
and that phrase was 'Made in Canada.'

47. Tonight's Episode: No Roman Holiday.

I like to just sit and watch cars pass by.
The Chevy logo is frequently worshipped
by snake handlers. 'Ferrari' means 'Hello'
in Italian. I am weary with L.A.

At the Alibi Room in Culver City,
I met with my snitch. He called me a jerk.
It surprised me that a paranoid narcissist
could remember such tiny-ass details.

We heard the ad for Tito's and felt better:
I love Tito's Tacos, you'll love Tito's too.
'It's not far from here,' the snitch said,
before ratting out an old college chum.

We sat in lawn chairs in the parking lot.
He tried to get a laugh ragging on my car.
'It's good for where I'm going,' I said,
dramatically pointing at the asphalt.

48. Tonight's Episode: Heaven is a Hellyard.

For better or worse, these are my catchphrases:
'In the end, it doesn't really matter,'
'What concerns me most is the joint pain,'
'Could I get extra hot sauce on the side?'

In the original pilot for *Happy Days*,
Fonzie's catchphrase was 'The sun is shining!'
Among friends, Eleanor Roosevelt's catchphrase
was 'Hot dogs 'n' pickles sure do tickle.'

At the launch for *The Old Gumshoe Dancer*:
The Memoir of Barnaby Jones, I said little.
Content to just get through it and smile,
happier to sign a few copies and then leave.

The fire never left me, it still burns unwise.
Even I'm surprised sometimes I can still move,
drive and duck a bullet or two. More surprised
that last bullet has yet to find me.

IV. North of Chicago

49. So, there I was, feeling better, no longer watching *Barnaby Jones*, but teaching in Illinois.

In the end, I had to go back to teaching.
I missed the apartment buildings and bookstores,
and by that I mean I needed the money.
Oh, St. Joseph's Community College!

American Fiction. I found it difficult.
Why should I stand in the way of some kid's dream
of being a dental hygienist because
I didn't like their thoughts on *The Great Gatsby?*

I lived by myself in a one-room flat,
near a row of gas stations, about
seven miles north of Chicago. I loved
the Cubs like a good late-life lunatic.

I cut my hair very short and I was
white with lots of bald. I looked like Wallace
Stevens, if Stevens ate more often at Wendy's.
In the end, I had to go back to teaching.

50. Welcome to the Wiener's Circle.

I shed the heaven-nodding politeness
of the South and squared my shoulders again.
Chicagoans took pleasure in being brusque –
what was there to be so nice about anyway?

I chinned up as winter iced the lakeshore,
never interested in reading your manuscript;
I watched golf and bit-torrented *Entourage*,
swearing at missed putts and not much else.

From grey head to yellow toe, I was me.
Whatever that means. I mean I suppose
John Dos Passos remained John Dos Passos
but I still wasn't reading his trilogy.

Chicagoland hot dog stands are open late.
'What the fuck you want?' one cashier asked me.
What the fuck *did* I want? Hope? A car? To write?
Jesus, I knew: just give me a Pepsi.

51. Falling Asleep to Beyoncé.

'Since I'm not your everything, how about
I'll be nothing?' A planned sobriety
ended at the Old Town Ale House
as I pretended to appreciate jazz.

For nearly a month the top thing I did
was drink Diet Sprite and listen to Beyoncé
in bed. Then, my dear Scooby, perfect pretty,
helped me give names to paintings in the bar:

Sailor Finger-Fuck, Gang Bang, Marilyn Snatch,
Bar Grope, Honey I'm Home, Camel Toe,
Lesbian Spread-Eagle, Bend Over Garter,
Fucked on the Bar, Old Perv and *Bronson Pinchot.*

Caught in my nacho cheese of conception,
caught in Old Navy khakis of necessity,
caught in Clairol Herbal Essence of love,
caught in the stammering staples of Ol' Stupid.

52. Once I wanted to be an astronaut, now I wear a housecoat.

The self-help book, carefully underlined
(browsed at 4 a.m. over the internet),
was fairly direct: just give it up, moron –
and so broke the moonlight on my face.

It may have taken four pestering texts,
but my best friend finally responded:
'I don't think it's true, but do what you want.'
Sweet validation of individualism.

To spend the rest of life riding a sofa,
telling one group I was working on
my novel, another that I was working
on my Civil War novel *Born Asunder*.

This is what happens when you stop crying
and consider the real pain of others:
you lie down and let them eat at Arby's.
No more Bronco Berry Sauce for you, moron.

53. A change of plans in light of spiritual contemplation and the purchase of new shoes.

'I will build a church out of the condoms
I once hoped to use!' I prayed to St. Joe.
'Joe, help me remember your full name –
the spelling mostly, I will fake the rest.'

Alone and silent-movie mistake-prone,
it was a good time to get God on side.
My legs had gone the way of Dillinger
and it was a chore to read Frank Norris.

McTeague, the dentist Democrats still fear,
could never tell bluebells from cowslip.
The one thing my modest tenure taught me
was September is a time for modest hope.

Back to the temple, Mount Prophylactica.
Forgiveness for neck punching is holy.
Forgiveness for fatalism is holy.
Forgiveness for blue Nikes is forthcoming.

54. Wake House.

The campus chapel, Wake House, looked more like
a clinic. A glass door, a foyer full
of pamphlets, four pews, wall-to-wall carpet,
but with a gold cross and a college-crested lectern.

I passed it when I went to the real clinic
(a pathology was being 'monitored'),
and I never saw worshippers, not even
a pale sophomore praying she wasn't pregnant.

I imagined myself walking into Wake House
and praying, on my knees, to Jesus Christ;
to mouth the words of surrender yet still
making my way, at night, to my bar.

Faith would be my dirty little secret,
a red lamp flame that would keep me going
as I prattled on about Nathanael West
and confirmed the bumper stickers of the day.

55. Pamphlet from Wake House: 'Living the Doctrine' (Reformed Latter-Day Doctrine).

Accept you do not change the course of the sun.
You did not create fluoride or *Maxim*.
You are not responsible for hosiery.
Accept your breakfast mistakes stoically.

Work on living a more righteous life.
Store your Samuel Clemens podcasts wisely.
Never fail to point out the Don Knotts scene.
Work on life's predictable sleep patterns.

Beware of Vail and the cranberry cures
that care nothing for your true happiness.
Keep your colanders handy around dusk.
Beware of loving Bud Light commercials.

Be a Star. Shoo away the hobo stains.
Don't read reviews that begin with the words
'I am plotting to blackball this writer.'
Be a Star. The starry emoticon.

56. Celery soup at O'Hare Airport.

Like all fine cuisine, airport celery soup
achieves *balance*. A strong sodium base
is complemented by briny accents
and salt is added to meld its flavours.

Perhaps it needed some anchovy paste,
a few chunks of Kentucky country ham.
And maybe the rim of the soup bowl
could be have been salted like a margarita.

I took the El but I was still too early
to meet you at the gate. Nearly two years
since I had seen anyone from home.
What besides airport soup to celebrate?

So, there we were, two small people
without much to talk about besides books.
You went off to a conference in the Loop.
I even got off a few stops early.

57. I did punch that guy in the neck, but it was the last game of the year at Wrigley and, in my defence, he did say, 'Wait till next year!'

Portnoy masturbating in a ballglove
was, I explained, 'the heart of America.'
All the dying father Rip Van Winklies were
wadded up in transcendentalism.

'A good day for a ballgame – let's play two!'
Mr. Cub said, and I agreed wholeheartedly.
Esp. if you replaced the words 'a ballgame'
with 'six-hour stand at Cubby Bear Tavern.'

J. Henry Waugh's stratomatic *Moby Dick*,
where Ahab becomes a beloved clutch hitter,
proved impossible to teach. From a cot,
at the back of the bar, I stab at thee!

The biggest cut can still go 6-4-3.
Trying is the most insignificant thing.
Each breakfast, each class, each marathon sesh,
each wrong-number exchange – you have to win.

58. That's right, grading papers is harder than working in the slaughterhouses described in Upton Sinclair's *The Jungle*.

The focused labour in an early piece
by Hemingway; a trapline followed through,
dappled light and neck sweat accounted for –
I lost that kind of buzz a long time ago.

I talked to my friend Meg about a new hire,
telling her he was a bit 'like me.' She said,
'So, he's also barred from taking
any free brewery tours in Missouri?'

We then imagined New Hire zipping through
stacks of papers, winking at St. Ignace
every time he patiently explained
the difference between *its* and *it's*.

Meg took yoga to help prevent burnout,
while I just prayed I would wake up younger.
I also pretended I didn't care
about the words intoned at choir practice.

59. O Little Star of Bethlehem, I would spank your pussy too.

The presentation on 'Comets that Kill'
was hours long. Has anyone ever
stayed awake for a planetarium show?
The tinsel stars for Christmas had come out.

The core temperature of Neptune's so cold
you can't build sex motels on its surface.
But, by the icy shores of Lake Michigan,
there's miraculous savings on cough syrup.

The sun swallows comets like french fries,
God smashes the wax cup once he's done.
Freedom fries, I mean, and the freedom wax cup.
Christmas Eve, a crossword, McDonald's.

If you're offered the choice of McNuggets
with a wish-granting genie and McNuggets
without a wish-granting genie, please
take the ones with the wish-granting genie.

60. Congratulations, poet, for referencing mangoes as a metaphor of sexual fulfillment for maybe the millionth time, you have won our hearts and souls and we have decided to name the Library of Congress after you.

The greatest thing about American fiction
is that for every great novel there's a movie.
It may not be a very good movie, mind you,
but they do spare one the chore of reading.

Yul Brynner starred as Jason Compson
in a film version of *The Sound and the Fury*.
Jerry Orbach starred as Freddy Exley
in a version of Exley's *A Fan's Notes*.

Demi Moore as Hester Prynne was sexy.
In the San Fernando Valley version,
Demi Moore is played by Ashlyn Gere
and she doesn't even get pregnant!

The silent movie version of *Typee*
is excellent as there's no talking –
but there are some frames that require reading
even if the frames are shorter than poems.

61. On the positive side, I went ice fishing in Michigan's Upper Peninsula.

Out of the top ten tourist attractions
in Michigan's Upper Peninsula,
three are ferries to Mackinac Island
and two are museums about shipwrecks.

Every single county in the U.P.
lists snowmobiling as a recreation.
Ads on radio warn seniors about grandkids
raiding and selling their prescription stash.

The folkloric character 'the Yooper'
is, essentially, an *eh*-saying Canuck.
Yooper humour has good riffs on hunting
and on parsnip-filled Cornish pasties.

'The edibility of tommy cod, eh,
depends on the taste of Lake Superior.'
On top of the ice, I phoned my mother,
who recommended the Mackinac Bridge.

62. I got more Appomattoxes than Ford Madox Ford has Fords.

After choir practice we would drink beer
at a Rush Street joint called Sudsy Malone's.
We were like our very own *St. Elmo's Fire*,
except with limper hair and wire-rim glasses.

Invariably I'd get tipsy enough to joke:
'Say what you will, the Mormon Tabernacle
Choir is one hostie tabernacle choir.'
Nobody listened but I liked it that way.

How was I to know, two summers later,
I'd take off to Nashville with the disgraced
soprano to write radio jingles
while she pursued her dream of hostessing.

Melville's Civil War poems are so correct
their insights seem like cribs: he would never write,
as I would, 'If Robert E. Lee ate tacos
you know he'd eat Music City Tacos!'

63. The power lifts me or, at least, fills me with the kind of false hope that will lead to a change of scene and, then, again, a familiar sense of despair.

I keep thinking it was Fitzgerald who
quit drinking when really it was O'Neill.
I know John Huston played 'The Lawgiver'
in *Battle for the Planet of the Apes.*

I knew less about the Christian rock
business in Nashville. I'd just have to learn
to avoid saying things like *God* or *Christ*
in favour of *The Power or The Light.*

'What do I care for Caesar's anger?
Let me give you a taste of mine!' Two spells
in Bridgeport taverns were embarrassing
and I've acquiesced to most things since then.

Why not just sit in a wooden chair
and strum guitar all afternoon? Neighbours
at work, nothing to read, nothing to drink.
Just a simple song to sing about floor wax.

64. The day before New Year's Eve.

The Ferris wheel at the Navy Pier
pulses candy light the night before
New Year's Eve. My joy limited to
screaming, 'That's offside!' at the TV screen.

I used to like the Bears. I used to winter
with the complete works of William Faulkner.
I have some friends around St. Joe's but can't
bear the smooches that precede 'Auld Lang Syne.'

Holding hands in a cab, cuddling on an old couch:
were those my only accomplishments in life?
I could still rhyme 'Get your life togezza'
with 'Say what you will, I love mozzarella.'

Trucking on, the sun'll still be bright
and the moon will still push the tides.
And when Natalie Imbruglia sings 'Torn,'
Natalie Imbruglia will still seem torn.

V. Nashville Songs

65. A Song for Lotion, a Song for Ointment.

Tell me I'll die in a towering inferno
and Steve McQueen won't save me from the flames.
I'll say goodbye like a gas-sniffing moron
and carve our initials on my hollow leg.

We're as different as lotion and ointment –
whatever that means, honey, is lost on me.
But like *fog* and *haze* or like *corn* and *maize*,
sometimes you've got to choose.

Into the void I'll take my Sears credit card
just so I will regret their swimwear sales.
I'll say hello to Festus from *Gunsmoke*
and he'll tell me Miss Kitty was just the same.

We're as different as lotion and ointment –
whatever that means, honey, is lost on me.
But like *glam* and *posh*, like *pumpkin* and *squash* –
sometimes you've got to choose.

66. Song To Rescue Us (and by Us I Mean Me) from the Good Intentions of Others.

The only song that matters is Faith Hill's
version of the *Sunday Night Football* theme.
Still, I have my Telecaster pleasures
as certain as waking up in Kansas.

I regret passing up on free tickets
to see Crinkle, Mudgut and the Hants Crew.
All those times I was 'Maybe Attending,'
I admit I wasn't going to attend.

Schubert's vomiting and swollen fingers
may have been from mercury poisoning –
not because he invented a new shooter
that he tried to market as the Trout Kiss.

Showing no care for unsexy neighbours,
I play AC/DC on mandolin.
I also admire Hank Williams, Jr.
doing the *Monday Night Football* theme.

67. Song for the Power that Watches over Us and also Reminds Us, from Now On, To Celebrate Milestone Birthdays with a Series of Invasive and Humiliating Medical Exams.

Bring on the Carpathia – *what else now?*
The plot to *Logan's Run* is everyone
willingly agrees to die when they turn thirty.
At that age, I still liked Cap'n Crunch.

When I was thirty-five I had a small stroke
and for a brief time time dollar signs
appeared to me as question marks –
so I thought you had won the lottery.

At forty-six I said I was forty-five:
walking from apartments that smelled like soup,
getting into fights in downtown taverns,
living mainly off gyro burgers.

Just sail on, Horatio Magellan Crunch,
there'll be no more birthday parties for me.
Chop the almond tree for a new canoe
and let me drift on the zero-calorie sea.

68. Song for Cardigans and Assholes.

It wasn't the smell of sage and honey
but a popular conditioning shampoo.
It wasn't a breeze coming from the east
just some girl yelling about Costco.

It's fine, I'm good, I drink Sierra Mist –
no need to introduce that grad student.
I know who he is and what all this is,
I'm not staying to talk about Foucault.

It wasn't the sound of a dying swan
but the gross tears of gross alcoholics.
It wasn't the taste of gunpowdered dawn
but leftover green beans and fish sticks.

It's fine, I'm cool, I'm not talking to you,
I thought you moved to San Francisco.
I pictured you there around Union Square
your sweater a bucket by your ankles.

69. Sea Shanty.

I got in some good whaling today.
I got in some pretty good whaling.
Or, at least, that's what I think I did –
I know there's a harpoon in my back.

A man pays a price for singing to mermaids:
$25 a song, $30 with contact.
The cross-Atlantic ho-hum, a free buffet,
The Rush Limbaugh Show piped into my cabin.

Sea sponges and Yorkshire pudding specials
at the Suckfish Tavern on Bishop Street
where I, with Erin the Red, vikinged away
a whole winter and six whole paycheques.

'Great Whaling Jobs!' The kind of whaling jobs
that would see my parents sit the Joneses to tea
and say, 'My boy's aboard the *Coarsewind*!'
and I am, Ma, Da, ready to puke when I see land.

70. D-Lux Song.

Hell is other people's taste in music.
For three years now, I've had this tune
in my head. I think it goes, 'Beazy, Beazy,
Beazy, let your hair be a shade of brown.'

Hell is other people's taste in music.
I counted the songs the folksinger sang,
from 'Hello, Doveflight' to 'The Coal-Light Song' –
who knew there were twenty of them?

Hell is other people's taste in music.
Try a road trip with a Frank Zappa fan
or tell your new love you fall asleep
listening to *The Well-Tempered Clavier*.

Hell is other people's taste in music.
For five years now, I've had this song
in my head: 'With or without you, I'm cool,
totally going to L.A. either way, babe.'

71. Song for a Silent Treatment.

I told her, in plain language, how I felt.
And by that I mean I mumbled a poorly
paraphrased and already cryptic passage
from one of Yeats's later poems.

When she asked, 'What was that?' I said, 'Nothing.
Nothing. It doesn't matter.' It mattered,
of course. '*Ma vie est usée. Allons, feignons …* '
On second thought, it doesn't matter at all.

The fuel in the sun is finite. It must be.
But I guess I won't think that in L.A.
I'm inattentive the way a husband is –
confident there's always tomorrow.

Warm July wind in the downtown square
where the U.S. bible industry's located.
Your hair blowing about, not saying much,
the last time someone seemed happy to see me.

72. Song for *The Blue-Hinded Hive.*

She wanted to be with her own kind:
experimental theatre and boxed wine.
Downloading movies, hiding from the sun,
she said, 'This couldn't be any better.'

I remembered her from that downtown bar,
all her friends talking about 'the cinema.'
She looked like Patricia Kalember;
she said she liked how I hated everyone.

She wrote a book called *The Blue-Hinded Hive*,
I never asked what on earth that could mean.
Wobbly on our feet from vodka and lime,
we yelled into the pit of an alley.

She wanted to be with her own kind:
open mic Sundays and Four Loko chugging.
Not that I complained about a sandwich;
not that the sandwich was love all the same.

73. Song about the Rod Stewart Impersonator/Blackjack Dealer I Lost One Hundred Dollars to, Left on Alex Parker's Answering Machine at the Imperial Palace Casino in Las Vegas, Nevada.

Micropress manner is the metameme,
I like country clubs: golf's a great game.
I like how the *o* in 'ocean' stands up.
LOL, smiley icon. You can go fuck yourself.

In *Sister Carrie*, Carrie shop-window-peeks
and turns to Samantha and says, 'Hey, ho,
you couldn't possibly be with the Poet?'
Dissertating can lead to great weight gain.

The method for poetry is like dance:
you get drunk with your idiotic friends
and refuse to do it. The Qu'ran states,
'OMG, bad sitch, coming to you now.'

Rebecca Black's 'Friday' is a better song
than Bruce Springsteen's 'The Rising.'
Fond of airplane travel, are you? Laptops
are on sale just outside, just like lemonade.

74. Song for Mid-Season Cancellations.

I'd been watching a DVD collection
of the first season of *thirtysomething*.
The parts about Elliot and Nancy
felt too real to even sit through.

The only character I strongly identified
with was Michael's dad. He wore a toupee
and gruffly talked through his desire to plant
a maple tree just before he falls to cancer.

I imagine maple leaves everywhere in the streets
of Montreal at this time. It's too cold
to sit outdoors, apartment heaters are on,
people talk of how bad the hockey team is.

I try to schedule a routine in my mind –
so many hours reading and writing,
some for guitar. I have a new song!
'Put the Man in Manipulate and Turn Around.'

75. Song of December.

Thanks to the plentiful white space in ads
for American Apparel on the back page
of the *Scene*, I wrote my worst songs:
'Little Gunny' and 'Calling all Denverites!'

References to sports teams can be changed
to fit marketplace. Even though, I argued,
almost being stabbed by an Eagles fan
is not the same when it's a Colts fan.

Nashville stripclubs sprout by the highway
where, I imagine, many have worked/danced,
waiting out the most difficult stretch
in their quest to be the next Taylor Swift.

I started a Christmas song with the lyric
'My feet still wet from that Montreal rain.'
Gah! I was leaving. Those who think you can't run
away from your problems just haven't tried.

76. Song that Formerly Used the Quote, ‘Let Go, It’s Over – Nobody Listens to Techno!’

Familiar afternoon light of the mall,
hiding some of January away.
I keep buying the wrong shoes, wrong shoehorns.
Riding a bench with a venti Pike Place.

I miss Muzak – its fine orchestrations.
Now, even ambient background music
is basically the same tunes spun at night
by ambitious DJs at loft parties.

This year, I’ll spot the dogwood blossoms.
It’s written down in my new agenda –
the one I hope not to lose in a cab along
with its scribbles about a ‘last darkness.’

First, a military salute to resolution.
Yogourt fine as vanilla ice cream.
The most amazing long-distance savings,
tomorrow and tomorrow at the mall.

77. Song of Acceptance.

When Elvis Presley rides around the world
on his lucky mule, Burt, to cure villages
of their most stubborn and unproductive coughs,
don't you get he's also thinking about you?

Remember when you wrote one hundred poems
and each one was rejected, on first view,
from journals like *Caveborn*, *Binzah* and *Wakings*?
Elvis loved those poems. He really did.

He even read the one about your first love,
Highlighting the phrase, 'how death's little pinky
tickles you,' just to cruelly keep you alive.
Elvis just wants you to be happy.

When Elvis is planning river clean-ups,
bracing locals for what smart people say,
it may be easy to feel small. But even Burt
doesn't stamp by the pistachio trees.

78. Song after Verlaine.

The piano I bashed in your rec room
until it couldn't make a tin can's sound,
pre-dawn, early March, will never be fixed.
'This song is for all my obviousness!'

Then came the vodka and Diet Sprite drinks
and riding the sofa's wave just like Duke
Kahanamoku. I worked at Quiznos –
why did you still tickle the ivory?

Why 'Piano Man' and the hard clang
of tourist change? I had crazy hair then.
What did you want besides crazy hair
and a guy who set fire to cop cars?

The piano I bashed in your rec room,
as you cried along to its last harmonies.
Without an axe, without a baseball bat,
as I sang, 'Take Me Out to the Ballgame.'

79. Song of the Hummingbird.

When you get older you hear the word 'lance'
more often as a verb than as a noun.
You may be okay because you did something,
but sad because you know God has the last lance.

It was sad, like one of those episodes
of *Will & Grace* when the actors 'act.'
Or the time I thought a Perry Ellis golf shirt
would make me look less bosomy.

I've quietly darted from bush to bush.
I've written exacting, insulting letters
that I thought were unimpeachable.
Who knew the word 'blowsy' could hurt so much?

Hummingbirds do not live to be fifty,
nor do they edit e-magazines.
Their lance-shaped beaks pierce the honeysuckle,
and the honeysuckle blooms coral bright.

80. Song of the Mermaid.

Henry Hudson and John Smith both claimed
to have seen mermaids en route to America.
Was it so far-fetched Sasha Grey would come
to me and whisper, 'Poetry's a joke?'

The mermaid Thessalonika would ask,
'Is King Alexander alive, and, really,
does he need to be such a drama queen?'
And then she would make octopus wine.

In James Cameron's blockbuster *Aquaman*,
there's a scene where Aquaman (Vincent Chase)
saves a mermaid from paparazzi, fame
being antithetical to living underwater.

The word 'mermaid' is Old English, it means
Don't ask me to solemnize my zipper.
And so I have sang my last country song
for the mermaid – I mean *done sung*.

VI. L.A.

81. Manhattan Beach.

The pier lights come on as the sun dips down.
Pelicans make their last swoops to the sea
and California is happy for evening.
Come to the sports bar and pound some Bud!

Orange light and early retirement,
a small crowd half-heartedly cheering Kobe,
sensing some sadness in the inevitable –
where impossible three-pointers are common.

'What are your next ten labours, Hercules?'
It will be dark when the hot wings are done,
and the bar's Dave-Matthewsy playlist
will remind us of an unchanging drear.

Silly, let's recall our once-golden state
as the sound of police helicopters
whirr overhead and a liquor store fracas
echoes, unresolved, long into the night.

82. Santa Monica.

Primrose and birds of paradise. Ten
minutes into L.A., *tacos de trompa* woozy.
A seaside bar – peanut husks and sawdust –
Greta Scacchi canoodles with a younger man.

Soft Pacific blue and pink adult superstores.
Candy colours of the rides on the pier.
Bogus cantinas: *Harvey Mex, Senor Tequila.*
Starbucks, Auntie Anne's Pretzels and Old Navy.

The clinic is on the third floor of the mall.
A doctor sits down before speaking of death,
but people stand to ask: 'Cash or credit?'
'A pathology is a pathology.'

Should have got that dog: the terrier who'd
rip through underwear drawers unscolded.
Even Dodge Caravans can't go back in time,
but Dodge Caravans remain ever true.

83. The Merle Haggard of Culver City.

Glumlog, Scarlet Lady Saloon, August.
Hal, the cursing beer pong champ,
pointed out a cracked Miller Lite mirror:
'That mirror is more fattening and tastes worse.'

Lady's 'celebrity anecdote night'
again drags as yet again the winner
concludes with a note about asking for gum
from a tipsy Dwayne 'The Rock' Johnson.

But then, Lady's 'country open mic night'
picks things up when the chorus goes:
'Cute as a squirrel wearing pyjamas
with prints of squirrels wearing pyjamas.'

Of course, nobody asks to go canoeing.
Nobody asks if there was some activity
that can help rebuild what was ruined.
'Lady, I'd rather die than do yoga.'

84. From Simi Valley to Malibu to Maui.

Orange trees and sage. A conference call
mercifully averted with a lame excuse.
'Getting shot hurts,' Ronald Reagan wrote
in his journal in April of '81.

It's clearly unfair to compare fortune
to John Hinckley, Jr., esp. when fortune
doesn't care as much for Jodie Foster.
Carsick through the canyons to Malibu.

Duke's, the chain resto named after surfer
Duke Kahanamoku, has Plexiglas
to protect drinkers from the wind,
making for a more pleasant Mai Tai nap.

The suicide fantasy starts in Malibu:
swimming out, saying, 'I'm going to Hawaii!'
Mental resos at the Waikiki Hilton,
which seems like a real hot spot to vaycay.

85. East on I-10.

Stover Ave. and Cherry. A sale
on Skoal at a K-Gas station. Biscuit
sandwiches and *cerveza helada*
pace out the day. Off to Las Vegas.

A former student back at St. Joseph
e-mails, 'Just how much abuse can you take?'
Winter rains darken the mountain passes,
and there's lightning towards Pomona.

There was supposed to be a turnaround.
To identify with a YA novel
protagonist. *Chester 'Chubs' Morrison*
is fifteen, overweight and into math.

Tobacco juice in an empty Popeyes cup.
Finding the sunny side of the mountains,
a little bit of light, some luck for the night –
just when that student may have his answer.

86. Oceanside.

Every new-to-Cali knob thinks the sunlands
will dry out the damp root of their eastern ache;
it's as ridiculous as movie scenes where men
jump off rooftops and don't end up in wheelchairs.

There's a simple logic to L.A.'s values.
People don't pretend your personality
is of consequence. The wisdom of
prostitution blossoms with magnolias.

Angelinos live like they believe people
only care about you for your money
or your tits. Life is more relaxed, relieved
of a grad student's sense of what is *fair*.

Brandy and plastic cups in the parking lot –
a little impromptu eucharist.
This is your body and this is your body –
a good chug for pretending you don't care.

87. The Dresden Room.

'Are you familiar with the Los Feliz scene?'
she asked, folding her arms. 'Neither am I.
Actually I've been hiding from it all
since I forgot the lyrics to "Octopussy."'

The sound of a cold April rain by morning,
wanting more than anything to leave
the envelopments of blankets and sleep
and be just another car swooshing through.

'Why don't we drive to Salt Lake City?'
A fairly drastic way of dealing with
one's reluctance to go to Hollywood bars
filled with ironic skinny-jeaned hipsters.

Like all sensible people who hate jazz,
the kindle of affection was in booze.
A coat over one's own head a hideaway,
the lyrics to 'Goldfinger' still kicking.

88. A parking lot in Canoga Park.

Afternoon sunlight. Potted bougainvilleas
around a Rite Aid. Drugstores still count on faith –
like little prayer booths where you may leave
with a spray foam that will lead to salvation.

The city's promised to let palm trees die.
They're a drain on precious water,
not even indigenous to L.A.
All too much for dollar-store sunglasses.

Napping in a '98 Toyota
is easier than having two roommates.
Eating canned tomatoes straight from the can
can be surprisingly elegant.

A car pulls in and the stereo starts to bump,
I got a date with Coco, date with Coco ...
A kid taps on the windshield just because.
The bougainvilleas are geraniums.

89. Popular inscriptions on cakes in Los Angeles's Cake District around Fairfax.

- *The Butterfly Hairclip Came from Last Night.*
- *Enjoy Your Brief Victory, Cap'n Crunch.*
- *Might As Well Stop Talking About SoHo.*
- *Happy Birthday, Thanks for Buying this Cake!*

- *Right Now, I Am Giving You the Finger.*
- *For Today, Let's Just Call You Sweet Nimrod.*
- *Blow the Candles. I Want to See My Real Friends.*
- *Tonight is the Night I Smash Precious Things.*

- *Our Icing has an SPF of 8!*
- *Have a Nice Trip. Enjoy Your Self-Pity.*
- *Dead Father, Dead Father, blah, blah, blah, blah.*
- *Rolling on in Misery Has Rewards.*

- *I Really Don't Care if You Miss New York.*
- *Let's End Polio Really Soon, Okay?*
- *I Read Your Poem, the One About Knees.*
- *It's Not Like You're Some Hot Guy or Something!*

90. Rare periodical section, Duarte's Donuts, Santa Monica Blvd.

It's not hard to be tricked into something
even more absurd than a Ponzi scheme.
Dear Lord, let me get that part in *Ass Angel*,
help me become the best *Ass Angel* yet.

Then, gah, tweeting took too much energy.
A sun-bleached doughnut place in a strip mall
would serve well as a public library.
'Songwriter sees shadow on a lung.'

The age of mixed CDs and corner-store wine
has passed as certainly as the Bronze Age.
Some still lick the nubs of ballpoint pens,
some lose their passion for television.

Returning to Canada and its sofas
seemed inevitable. Returning home
to teach at James Buchanan High School –
the same school Leonard Cohen went to!

91. Zuma Beach.

Deep as a dumpster, fuzzy as a kiwi,
no more bragging about east-coast soups.
There are PhDs in creative writing
but it's different on *Planet of the Apes*.

Strong as Claritin, soft as pot noodles,
just pretend you live in a beer ad.
The buzz along the Pacific Coast Highway
sounds just enough like Shania Twain.

Open as Denny's, layered like a pizza box,
time to cash in on the demand for loafers.
Sand will not stick to our feet anymore.
Sunnyrest, Shady Oaks, Heavenly Pine.

Finished as Schubert's Eighth, done as *Jersey Shore*,
time to be nobody else's Frankenstein.
One phrase will resonate through the service:
It never happened. It never happened.

92. That's funny. Because in my other dream, Heidi Montag beats up a busboy.

Let me share my life philosophy:
never be in a place where the words
'oldest' and 'fattest' apply to you.
You can be one of those, just don't be both.

Somewhere between the spicy yucca fries
and gooseberry crostini, sleep came,
sure as the Grammy goes to the flautist
who recorded *Motorhead for the Flute*.

I dreamt you convinced me Pinocchio
was called Pinolio. Considering
the fights we'd have about *Archie* comics,
I was glad to accede it was Pinolio.

Hawthorne, avocados, cactus, Persian limes:
my mornings will certainly be sunny.
My Los Angeles will be sad without you.
Pinolio should never tell a lie.

93. The David Hasselhoff Boys Club

Mr. Hasselhoff, convenient whip welt,
floater in seven diabetic eyes,
our civil war docs competing, absent
of those handwritten 'quite beautiful' notes.

Mirror ape, afternoon sleep still smelling
of the last time rapini was left on the stove,
arguing politics with a sandwich –
mustard thinks it's the first campus lefty!

Leaving the door open rather than ask
anybody if they wanted to watch *Mannix*,
didn't anyway, Frankie Carbone hooked,
silent-treated me good again, Canada.

What else was to be expected, cancer fear?
Recognition laugh in the Hoff has Cub
Scout ask, 'Aren't you supposed to kill people
for the sake of poetry (I mean money)?'

94. Script ideas.

A Culver City sublet just to sit
and work all day on two ugly scripts:
The Brothers Pantoozi and *Adios,*
Debbie Johnson. Vodka and Red Bull.

The inspiration for Debbie Johnson
said, 'Meet me at Tom Bergin's on Fairfax.'
All the Flemish wheat and English cotton
overboard, not a stick of credit left.

'Debbie is older than I am,' she said,
yawning between gulps of Guinness.
'You wouldn't care about either of us!'
Still, she paid, and without much cursing.

'How could Arnold Rothstein have the patience
for pinochle?' one of the Brothers Pantoozi
says to another Brother Pantoozi.
Meaning it's a skill to learn to drink alone.

95. Sunset news.

Plastic draped the one newsstand on Sunset
in a quick summer downpour. Water rushed down
the hills, spouting up at the few sewers.
An ablution for my reading of Updike?

Flipped pages of *Jannahat*, just looking
for familiar names. As if those who read
with me years back on St. Lawrence Street
were gamely pecking L.A.'s little lit zines.

'I once thought you knew some oppressive truth
I desperately wanted to know. But now
I'd rather believe in Ontario:
Saturday hockey, cheap pizza and brew.'

The rain picked up and Humvees sped through.
Maybe the Dodge Caravan would appear,
just in time, and the doors would slide open.
And, like that, normal American sunshine.

96. LAX.

Even after someone put duck on pizza,
after someone put duck into a fish
and that fish was put into a sheep's stomach
then stuffed into an egg, people went hungry.

Coasting for a long time on just one skill –
the ability to start a fight
at a wedding reception – it was time
for a stretch of bad haircuts and silence.

Heckling comedians at the Troubadour,
faking heart attacks at the Viper Room,
standing in line at Genghis Cohen –
who wouldn't miss such sunshiney happiness?

Doing things because it makes you 'happy'
is the logic of the Lotus Eaters.
Now I like lotus more than most people,
but sometimes you have to do what's right.

VII. Ville-Marie

97. I blame you, Jacques Cartier.

In the end, I had to go back to teaching.
Cleaving the possessive from the plural,
returning to Montreal like Richler –
at the age one ought to slump to Florida.

Leonard Cohen stays in California,
where, it is my understanding, he works
developing jam flavours for Smucker's.
Love is a fire, apricots are sweet.

Poet's Corner in Ben's went with Ben's,
replaced by a much handsomer building
with spankier selections of Spanx, *ensuite*,
just another place but without Applebee's.

The river speaks to me in TV themes:
Join the wacky St. Lawrence and the gang
for laffs a-plenty in La Belle Province.
In the end, I had to go back to teaching.

98. Île Metropoledance.

And, of course, *Bienvenue à Montréal*,
the Quebec City of bigger cities,
the Windy Poutine, the nation's capital,
home of the St. Louis Cardinals.

Turtleneck vendor to the world,
quality astrology convention island,
where both *coffee* and *café* are overpriced
and served with a distinct Euro-sass.

Birthplace of the Denver omelette, cradle
of failed revenge plots, mother of Céline,
father of the sexclamation mark, oh yes,
and final resting spot of the *Nimitz*.

Where it didn't matter what Hamlet said,
if the dollar made you wish you were dead,
where I dunked my bagels into the wreck,
and I tweeted out a *hallellujah*.

99. Putting the 'ah' in 'adjunct.'

Creamy university press titles:
Stalking Abraxis: The Early Fiction
of Jenny Schecter. One is Too Many:
Alienation in Don Birnam's Fiction.

Respectful, serious, never caught mouthing
the words to 'Party in the USA.'
I say I wanted that more than anything –
but the Miley Cyrus disks speak for themselves.

I wasn't a full-time professor
but I still worked for the university.
I was a departmental mascot –
'Skewy' the Creative Writing Bee!

In that warm, itchy outfit for Skewy
I buzzed about the halls at big events.
I'd wave my arms and say, 'Show, don't tell,'
and, 'Your craft will set the world abuzzzzzzzzzz!'

100. A strange, unexplained trip to Boston.

The jostle and lurch of a twin-prop flyer.
Landing at Logan to a few smokes, the *Globe*,
and a strawberry glaze at Dinky Dee's.
I've always loved trying to run away.

Downtown Crossing in Boston. Winthrop's grave,
sandwich stands, hip-hop clothing and sports bars.
Daniel Webster, apparently, would polish off
six plates of raw oysters. Poor Mrs. Webster!

I told my editor, 'You know, Karen, California
is a wonderful place to die,' years
after the desultory sojourn to Los Angeles –
my desk in Montreal tidy as an exhibit room.

Student poems sit in two piles,
freshmen and advanced classes. The poems wait
with their dewy observances on love,
the goo of the body, and George W. Bush.

101. I also blame you, Radisson and Grosseliers – especially you, Grosseliers.

Snow clings to stairwells on Dorchester
as another January slips away.
I sleep late, lumpen, satisfied with life,
while my secretary lines up phone calls.

Or, I just sleep a-jitter, alone,
clutching a Disney souvenir notepad,
where, instead of noting rains, snows, hearts,
I've written nearly twenty Heath Ledger jokes.

I've outlived Poe, Rimbaud and Fitzgerald!
I've seen North Chicago and South Chicago,
and sometimes have been relatively unhaunted
by 'tha incident' out back of Sullivan's Tap.

Spring will begin on St. Patrick's Day:
beer will make it so. A greening will come
regardless of how the temperature might plunge;
well before Valentine's, I drank sugarpop.

102. July-O-My.

The Berlin Turnpike in Connecticut
was heaven with stops for potato chips –
heavenier. Tiger Woods, y'all –
nodding off to golf on a motel TV.

My grip on reality's a bit greased up,
starting to envy Nelligan's long stay
in Saint-Jean-de-Dieu mental hospital,
forty years after *La Romance du Vin.*

Lear's prison, the sensible egg-free cakes,
calling rehab 'camping.' Wanting to die
is also a weird, annoying callback,
like getting the measles as an adult.

Tu proverai sì come sa di sale
lo pane altrui. Reach for the fancy mayo,
mayo so fancy it puts an aura
around a sandwich even sinners can see.

103. May you be forever wrong.

The Underground City of Montreal,
basically a group of connected malls,
was where I shook off the pain of summer –
a notebook, a cold Coke, iPhone at home.

Technically too young to be a mall walker,
I still liked the idea of a tracksuit,
all white and Adidas striped, pristinely
covering what happened to my body.

People were so afraid of Constantine,
they were reluctant to move his dead body
for fear he'd be angry at them. History
proves no one has ossified into a statue.

History also proves there are some stains
that even Tide detergent can't erase.
Lady Macbeth might have liked Palmolive
but it was no cup of Tide for Deep Shame.

104. I never understood Celsius but I walked the streets of Montreal in October.

About thirty-five degrees Normalheit
and after midnight. Not a long walk
to where I'm headed but it feels like
I am somehow stuck in a canoe.

I pass a studenty apartment building
where I went to a college party
twenty-five years earlier dressed up as Joe
DiMaggio. Beers and shots of ouzo.

It once seemed so unbearably romantic,
the roses Joltin' Joe had delivered every day
to Marilyn's grave in Los Angeles.
How stoic and certain in such doomed love.

Now I think more, *Poor old Mr. Coffee.*
It must have cost a pretty penny
to have loved Mrs. Arthur Miller,
and impossible to vote Kennedy.

105. Still walking the streets of Montreal in October, still not getting Celsius, still not dressing well for winter.

I host a sports talk radio show
until midnight. I quickly forget
about my bad Mike Tyson impression
and almost all my on-air transgressions.

There are corner stores at every corner,
all with names that avow great savings:
Dépanneur Valu-Prix, Boni-Prix,
Dépanneur Economy, EZ-Prix.

I walk slowly, as if to absorb winter's cold,
rather than rush on out of fear.
I paw my cellphone like a rosary,
hoping a little mercy might buzz through.

That somebody would say, 'Great show tonight!'
even though I knew no one was listening.
'Hey, sports guy, way to call Guillaume Latendresse
Billy Tenderness. You are amazing!'

106. At some point, even in Montreal, you just stop somewhere and enjoy the fine art of sitting.

The bartender, my friend, calls me Doc.
He says, 'Doc, what's wrong? You don't seem like Doc.'
I tell him I'm fine but I made 'mistakes ...
and coming to this pub is one of the worst!'

I indulge him in an unwise metaphor,
saying it feels like a bandage protecting a sore
that long needed more serious attention
is slowly being torn off my skin.

He lets me smoke inside after the customers
are gone. We talk about baseball in the back.
I tell him I once saw a Montreal Expo
in the SuperSexe, too wasted to wash his hands.

I think of how heavy (happy) that Expo
looks now. I lost some weight four years ago,
and then I didn't act in quite the same way:
fastball gone, but good junk coming across.

107. The unspeakable beauty of it all.

I start to choke up marking papers.
The sincerity of the grade-grubbing
is so beautiful. Still, I understand
the job I was hired to execute.

My role is to evaluate fairly
and offer comments. Their role is to look
at their B-range grade and call me an 'ugly
pig' on ratemyprofessor.com.

I have long since learned to stand up and smile,
tell jokes and provoke, only to escape
into the unreachable squalor of my home
where I always keep the TV on.

The way McDonald's stopped calculating
how many hamburgers they have served,
I stopped counting the times I was called ugly.
It was a lot, so why advertise?

108. Manipulative, passive-aggressive, two-headed monster – with benefits.

We walked to Hochelaga-Maisonneuve
and saw a woman wrestled to the ground
by drugstore clerks, her belly and blue bra
exposed to everyone on the street.

You chewed lozenges, mediciney ones,
while I droned on about molasses and rum.
In the blue dark of a hospital ward
I compared us, at last, to *The Flintstones*.

We walked through Fletcher's Field
so many times we began to recognize
the dogs of people who lived nearby.
Everything said we should get a dog!

We walked to different cafés up the street.
I think it was up the street – not New York.
As our friends talked 'global enwarmening,'
the winter poem was, again, Montreal.

109. 'Aloha' means both hello and goodbye and it is an implicit critique of the social formations that collude to induct 'Ivy League style' (with the Sperry Top-Siders and Quoddy moccasins).

Eventually, putting aside my gripes
was a matter of tossing old poems –
with take-out menus and old syllabuses –
into a banker's box: 'Goodbye, Stinky!'

They could end up sending me to Paris,
but even if they don't, I won't mind.
I can find my own Champs-Élysées
by a train station in Schenectady.

Along a street where the only storefront
not boarded over is the office
of a public defender, I can sit out
the soft, hilarious parts of summer.

The GE factory is not hiring.
Angelina Jolie's not at a Wendy's.
But I will be gone, and there is no drink
as sweet as the sweet drink of leaving.

110. Exceptional foundationalism! The community! Free trip to France!

I read at a Council-sponsored event,
dead grateful for the invite and the fans.
I was paired with a poet from Ottawa
who clucked like a chicken for five minutes.

The very first print mention of my name
was in a column about how useless
poetry seemed to the failed novelist
who wrote the article for his friend's zine.

What 'spoken word' is is hard to define.
It's mysterious that a five-minute performance
often takes a half-hour to perform.
Sooner or later, though, all the clucking stops.

The spoken worders were nice to me, though,
much nicer than the poets who compared
rosemary to stones. 'Nice reading, Doctor,
gotta get my copy of *Chicken Stone* signed!'

111. ***L'Assomption.***

I finally saw my name in the credits
of *Adios, Debbie Johnson.* Graded
all the final exams with a half-mark bump.
'Why can't any of you little punks yodel?'

One full paid month at the *Auberge Versailles.*
When, really, it made no difference to me
if it was the Astro Motel in Waco.
Except the Astro did have free HBO.

Alors, there was the pestering worry
I'd have to sell all my fridge magnets,
even the one that said 'Hawg Wild in Hope,'
but I stored them all in nine souvenir mugs.

The mugs made me cry less than they used to.
I wanted every second of precious life
to be commemorated with trading cards
and a catchy theme song. So long, suckers!

112. The Umbrellas of Anjou.

Not quite Dwight D. Eisenhower. Walking
the working-class suburb where I grew up.
The oil refineries that sprouted there
in the Great Depression still process crude.

My parents' house, built in 1957,
in accordance to the low-slung tropes
of California, is still there, at the bus stop.
My father still tends to summer flowers.

I know how much fat mayors are hated,
I know how cherries and olives don't mix,
I know the solution to all problems
isn't watching reruns of *The Nanny*.

The shopping malls were built in the '60s
That is how I would eventually learn
the important things, like how *Paul Blart: Mall Cop*
is known in French as *Paul Blart: Flic du mail.*

VIII. The Fountains of Versailles

113. A thousand maiden stones aslant.

'The garden grounds and their orderly paths
would have otherwise been blackberry
brambles and duck marsh. A faint slope of river
valley, ice forest whorls.' *Place Versailles.*

'Marble and granite depositories,
perpendicular to swampland moorings.
Apollo's credit line finally maxed out
to pay for Dionysus's hangovers,' *etc.*

In the southeast court, where I took pictures,
stands L'Escobade's labour *Les Trois Grâces.*
Creativity, Charm and Beauty.
Still, no Starbucks – which is unforgivable.

Shadows of the lithe figurettes fell over
the foot-weary who sat at the fountain edge,
big shopping bags by their ankles, while I tried
to recall lyrics to a pop song once loved.

114. Versailles bus stop.

I loved my colleagues and their playful putdowns.
I loved the way they paid attention to clothes –
as if they never considered how their tunics
and smart pantsuits looked like upholstery.

Bienvenue au centre d'élégance.
I sat back and reflected upon the years
as I waited for *l'autobus Roi René.*
Enough spouting cupids and peeing putti!

'Adorned in splendid marble, and scattered
with decorative water fountains and soothing
luminescent, Versailles is pure pleasing elegance.
All give in to its distinctive appeal!'

I loved my colleagues' itemized grant requests
and their proud air of accepted defeat.
'I will need time to explore the culture.'
You can't buy Wrangler jeans at Versailles.

115. 'In revenge great honour we achieve.'

The husband holds a pink, the wife some fruit.
Quista te dono per amore bella. A coltsfoot
poultice stinking up my book bag. Falling from
crowds like the illegitimate child of a pope.

Once, a squirrel came into the house
and napped for hours on my unopened *Gazette*.
Now, Fame holds her sword more intently
and Cupid's that kid crying on a plane.

Our cartouche too good for blue earth. Our pretty
salver for our Giant Eagle shrimp cocktails;
our family crest (The Bloody Fist of Goncourt)
emblazoned on my jacket with fine ticking.

Our pricey majolica meant to depict
the beheading of St. Crespina showed
Snooki getting punched by that dude at Karma.
Square in the nose, it's worth remembering.

116. Place Versailles.

Bronze frolickers in copper fountains.
More copper fountains, more bronze frolicking.
Aztec in influence, or perhaps Bauhaus.
It's not really as garish as it sounds.

To assess the artistic merit
of Versailles is to consider the triumph
of two sexy lingerie shops competing
in a mall. *Oui! Versailles Pik-Nik Donut.*

There's a sound barrier by the highway now
as if the ghosts who live *au bout de l'île*
need to eat their apples free from noise
while they consider their office gossip.

The best thing to do to an enemy
is poison their supply of canned bean dip.
'I'm in Anjou!' I tell all my old friends
as if light years from dips of any kind.

117. I tweeze therefore I am.

If lettuce and tomatoes grew arms and legs
and fought, contrary to most opinion,
lettuce would emerge the victor. Last night,
you should know, I spared you this observation.

I have just come up with the greatest name
for a Beyoncé cover band: Beyond-Cee.
My impression of a British decorator
rests solely on the phrase 'These blasted shelves!'

A poem in my chapbook *Li'l Chappie*
called 'Humourtous' was a cogito claim,
just an indicator I was alive
while holed up with stacks of magazines:

'Your tweezers may give you a pinch,
Your waxing may cause you some pain,
But don't talk to me about cosmetic misery
Until you've shaved your balls on a train.'

118. *Le P'tit Général.*

A pastry for lunch, *galette alsacienne*,
living long enough to skip work in new ways.
Bientôt nous plomberons ... But, first, sleep
(while downloading episodes of Urkel).

I heard tire skids from the autoroute,
sometimes the clang from loose bricks dropping.
The neighbourhood smelled of crumbling facades
and I just danced around the yellow tape.

It was absurd to say it caused despair.
Certain despairs, like gluten allergies,
should only (suspiciously) affect white
middle-class women or Canadians.

Sometimes the little gestures speak loudest.
I, for one, received a nice greeting card:
the word 'Holiday' calmly scratched out
replaced by 'Life in Hell' in florid cursive.

119. Jesus loves you, but doesn't love-love you; I mean He thinks you're okay but He's going through some things now and is not interested in something more meaningful.

I am waiting for a Dodge Caravan,
much like I am waiting for Jesus Christ
to smite all those smug Boston Red Sox fans.
I wait and mouth the word 'bituminous.'

I tried to live the code of The Doctrine once
but ended up sending unwise tweets
to a book clubber in Des Moines who called
her favourite white horse 'Raymond Carver.'

She reminded me of my best self,
she reminded me to return phone calls.
She reminded me it's not really Italian
when I say, '*secreto stasho di porno.*'

By the doughnut stand in Versailles,
taking out lemon-powdered day-olds,
I cursed God for not giving me fashion sense
but praised him for the taste of Diet Coke.

120. Rejected titles for the novel I received taxpayer money to draft.

- *Yes, You're Hot. But English-Department Hot.*
- *His Friends Called him 'Lou.' Louis Quatorze.*
- *In Texas, It's Just Called Being Selfish.*
- The English Patient *Vs.* Predator.

- *The Conspiracy Theory of Buck Ford.*
- *Buck Ford, Championship Moustache Model.*
- *Buck Ford and the Continental Surprise.*
- *Buck Ford, Creative Writing Instructor.*

- *Song of American Eagle Outfitter.*
- *Song for Whoever Who Coined the Word 'Yooper.'*
- *Song for a Prayer for a Sunday Drunk Dial.*
- *Song for Debbie 'Adios' Johnson.*

- *Autumn in Paris, Winter in Moline.*
- *Let's Agree It's Awful and Shake On It.*
- *The Man Who Watched* Jaws *700 times.*
- *The Man Who Never Actually Saw* Jaws.

121. Buy me a pony, narcissism.

I was to research the renovations
Versailles went through in the early eighties:
the Bergerac Room shut forever to visitors,
but a better café in the North Court.

All the books stacked neatly on my desk,
feeling comfortable with the verb '*essai*,'
I ended up just going onto Google chat
and talking about writing with a friend.

I mean, going into a *Star Trek* chat room
just to huzzah the salt demon episode.
'Isn't that the story of all our lives?'
'As if you aren't ruled by fantasy!'

I know the Hall of Mirrors knows no shame.
The pragmatism of the dermatologist
is incumbent on a patient's make-believe.
I dare you to pretend acne will not kill you.

122. The argument for making the grey jay (or 'whiskey jack') the National Bird of Canada.

Considering the business three years ago,
it's like I walked away from a plane crash.
I want to say I still taste naphthalene but,
honestly, I only taste caramel.

Considering I actually did walk away
from a car crash once, only to go home,
make ramen noodles and fall asleep,
I was not waiting on better news.

My mother was in the hospital again
and most of my summer was spent walking
through the old neighbourhoods, up the hill,
washing my hands, going to her ward.

The grey jay does not migrate in winter,
my mother argued, they live in spruce
(more national than maple), mate for life,
and never fly too far from their food supply.

123. You may remember me from the unpublishable manuscripts *Matador By Evening* and *Goodbye, Unlovable Stepchildren*.

In the course of working on my novel
I lost three jobs and soured countless friendships,
faked two heart attacks, lost six cellphones,
and ate every bite of a seventy-two-ounce steak.

I do not regret my best achievements:
when I referred to Northrop Frye as 'dude,'
when I convinced a pretty girl in Cleveland
my actual name was the Duke of Earl.

I do, however, regret writing fiction.
'Tom went to the fridge and took out the eggs.'
I mean, who cares? Smash all those eggs, Tom.
Do something besides move to Burnaby.

My nights of a thousand lesser Gatsbies,
the Sun Also Blames George W. Bush,
I held her hand and she said, 'Nobody,
not even the rain, has such a hairy back.'

124. I've already lived my life.

Before the iPhone arrived, we lived like pigs,
barely able to resist fratricide.
I'm honestly amazed I survived before,
what with all that 'listening' to people.

When the flood of favourite apps came to me,
I let the flow take me where it wanted.
I could be anywhere, looking at pictures
of drunk people on the internet.

I could see the friend at the masquerade
and how some *HuffPost* thing was liked twelve times.
I could listen to that message, you know,
from the taxi with the laughing in the back.

Best of all, I could set the temperature
to Fahrenheit and pretend to be normal.
I hold my iPhone to my chest to pray
for the thousands of texts I've deleted.

125. Death be not proud but, really, who could blame you? I mean, c'mon, you're Death!

I hope I don't die of kidney disease,
but I have eaten a cookie the size
of a birthday cake, so I will not feign
surprise about my likely fate.

I hope I don't die of liver disease,
but I have seen East Delaware City
and Pittsburgh in my drunkest winter –
what more could I really expect from life?

Here's to the beers, not the ones shared with friends,
but the ones downed in Mexican bathrooms,
or raised high in naval cemeteries
and chugged alongside the Suez Canal.

To the beers during our business meetings,
the ones while attending vernissages,
private christenings and dance recitals
(as if one could kill the pain of dance recitals).

126. 'What Was That Poem?'

My mother asked me, 'What was that poem?'
It was Longfellow's 'My Lost Youth,' I think.
The answer was Longfellow often enough,
even though she never liked 'Evangeline.'

I talked to my mother on my cellphone
outside a grocery store in Philadelphia.
She asked me what I was buying, 'Was it dear?,'
and if I now liked football more than baseball.

It was the last conversation I ever had with her.
I told her I liked baseball to make her happy.
I knew she wasn't calling to talk sports.
She was showing off, saying, 'I'm going to be okay!'

'What was that poem?' she'd say and act surprised
when I didn't know. It wasn't about the answer.
It was about noticing something held on to,
with wit and ferocity, until the day is done.

127. My life as a Canadian writer.

My first short story, 'The Provincial Fair,'
was rejected twenty-five times before
it found its home in the *Muskoka Review*.
From then on it's all been smooth sailing.

I learned the beauty of socialism
from writers so passionate they'd cry
when they didn't get a grant. We'd go north
and laugh at the thought of Alden Nowlan.

Yes, I have been on the radio!
If you heard that segment of *Canada Reads*
where a guy recommends the novel version
of Tom Cruise's *Top Gun*, that was me.

Now I live and work in Montreal.
All we do is sit in cafés and talk through
the one remaining question of literature:
is it available for free on the internet?

128. Or, just follow me on Twitter!

My lies were a more oafish Caliban. Mine,
but with just enough cursed independence
to rebuke their creator. Still, I stand by
my early sequence, 'Sonnets for a Dunce.'

Now that the red door to the Suckfish Pub
is closed, I think of the MGM Grand,
home to the last Sigma Derby electro-
mechanical horse-race table in Vegas.

All the thoroughbred races in summer,
all the new back-to-school Facebook friends.
Bless the bookmaker who gave me odds on
George Orwell's last tubercular visions.

I tell you I am running marathons,
dreaming up lemon-lime dental floss,
going in circles while my love cheers on.
Even Secretariat took the whip.

The time has come, the Walrus said, to talk of many things.

In loving memory of my mother, Mary Macdonald McGimpsey. Thanks to brothers Mike and Johnny; sisters Kathy, Karen, Janice, Gail and Heather; to my father John; and to Carol, as always, sunshine. Highest gratitude for Alana Wilcox, Kevin Connolly, Evan Munday and everyone on the Coach House team. Thanks to Elizabeth Bachinsky, Arjun Basu, Jeremy Breen, Steve Creep, Jon Paul Fiorentino, Deanna Fong, Scott Macdonald, Sarah Steinberg and Andrea Stevens. Special thanks to Jason Camlot, whose advice and friendship has been of immeasurable value while finishing these poems, and to Alessandro Porco, who read a very early version of this book with good humour and cool insight for which I'll always be grateful. I acknowledge the generous support of the Canada Council for the Arts. Poems from this book originally appeared in *Branch, Matrix, New American Writing* and *The Walrus*.

About the Author

David McGimpsey was born and raised in Montreal. His previous collection, *Sitcom*, was a finalist for both the A. M. Klein Award and the ReLit Award and was named by the *Quill & Quire* as one of 2007's 'Books of the Year.' David has a PhD in English Literature and is the author of the critically acclaimed and award-winning study *Imagining Baseball: America's Pastime and Popular Culture*. David writes a regular humour column called 'The Self-Esteem Workout' for *Matrix* and the 'Sandwich of the Month' column for *EnRoute* magazine. David is a songwriter and musician, and member of the rock band Puggy Hammer. In addition to being the author of one collection of short fiction (*Certifiable*), David is the Montreal fiction editor of the e-magazine *Joyland* and is the fiction editor for the Punchy Writers Series at DC Books. David was named by the CBC as one of the 'Top Ten English-Language Poets in Canada' and his work was the subject of the recent book of essays, *Population Me: Essays on David McGimpsey*. David currently teaches creative writing and literature at Concordia University.

Typeset in Gamma
Printed and bound at the Coach House on bpNichol Lane

Edited by Kevin Connolly
Cover and interior designed by Evan Munday
Photo of author (pictured with Scarlet Foxx and
Sophie Fatale of Hot Sludge) by Lynn Crosbie

Coach House Books
80 bpNichol Lane
Toronto, Ontario M5S 3J4

416 979 2217
800 367 6360

mail@chbooks.com
www.chbooks.com